DISCOVERING THE UNITED STATES

Washington

BY BLYTHE LAWRENCE

Kids Core
An Imprint of Abdo Publishing
abdobooks.com

abdobooks.com

Published by Abdo Publishing, a division of ABDO, PO Box 398166, Minneapolis, Minnesota 55439. Copyright © 2025 by Abdo Consulting Group, Inc. International copyrights reserved in all countries. No part of this book may be reproduced in any form without written permission from the publisher. Kids Core™ is a trademark and logo of Abdo Publishing.

Printed in the United States of America, North Mankato, Minnesota.
052024
092024

THIS BOOK CONTAINS RECYCLED MATERIALS

Cover Photo: Sean Pavone/Shutterstock Images
Interior Photos: Bettmann/Getty Images, 4–5; Danita Delimont/Shutterstock Images, 7 (top left); Abbie Warnock-Matthews/Shutterstock Images, 7 (top right); Thomas Hagenau/Shutterstock Images, 7 (bottom left); Ramil Gibadullin/Shutterstock Images, 7 (bottom right); Roman Khomlyak/Shutterstock Images, 8; Kris Holland/Yakima Herald-Republic/AP Images, 10–11; Edgar Samuel Paxson/IanDagnall Computing/Alamy, 12; Shutterstock Images, 13, 16, 24; Christian Petersen/Getty Images Sport/Getty Images, 15; VDB Photos/Shutterstock Images, 17; Valentyn Volkov/Shutterstock Images, 18; iStockphoto, 20–21, 25; Sean Pavone/Shutterstock Images, 22; Paula Dillinger/Alamy, 23; Dene Miles/Shutterstock Images, 27; Red Line Editorial, 28 (top left), 29 (top); Jeff Goulden/iStockphoto, 28 (top right); Joel Rogers/Corbis Documentary/Getty Images, 28 (bottom); Sergii Figurnyi/Shutterstock Images, 29 (bottom)

Editor: Christa Kelly
Series Designer: Katharine Hale

Library of Congress Control Number: 2023949377

Publisher's Cataloging-in-Publication Data

Names: Lawrence, Blythe, author.
Title: Washington / by Blythe Lawrence
Description: Minneapolis, Minnesota: Abdo Publishing, 2025 | Series: Discovering the United States | Includes online resources and index.
Identifiers: ISBN 9781098294182 (lib. bdg.) | ISBN 9798384913450 (ebook)
Subjects: LCSH: U.S. states--Juvenile literature. | Washington (State)--History--Juvenile literature. | Western States (U.S.)--Juvenile literature. | Physical geography--United States--Juvenile literature.
Classification: DDC 973--dc23

All population data taken from:
"Estimates of Population by Sex, Race, and Hispanic Origin: April 1, 2020 to July 1, 2022." *US Census Bureau, Population Division*, June 2023, census.gov.

CONTENTS

CHAPTER 1
The Great Seattle Fire 4

CHAPTER 2
The People of Washington 10

CHAPTER 3
Places in Washington 20

State Map 28
Glossary 30
Online Resources 31
Learn More 31
Index 32
About the Author 32

It took about a year to rebuild after the Great Seattle Fire.

The Great Seattle Fire

On June 6, 1889, a fire started in the basement of a woodworking shop in Seattle, Washington. The floor was covered in woodchips. The flames spread quickly. At that time, most buildings were made of wood. Soon, nearby buildings were on fire.

It took firefighters more than 12 hours to put out the flames. By that time, 25 city blocks had been reduced to ash. Nobody died in the fire. But much of the city was destroyed. The event became known as the Great Seattle Fire.

The people of Seattle had to rebuild many of the city's buildings. Slowly, a new city rose from the ashes. A few months later, Washington became the forty-second US state. The newly rebuilt Seattle would become one of its most important cities.

Washington's Land

Washington is in the West region of the United States. Canada borders the state to the north.

Washington Facts

DATE OF STATEHOOD
November 11, 1889

CAPITAL
Olympia

POPULATION
7,785,786

AREA
71,298 square miles
(184,661 sq km)

STATE BIRD

Willow goldfinch

STATE TREE

Western hemlock

STATE FLOWER
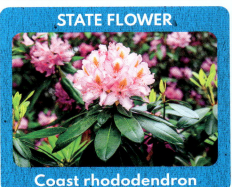
Coast rhododendron

STATE SPORT
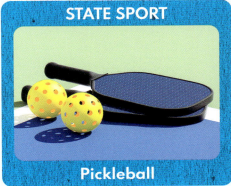
Pickleball

Each US state has a different population, size, and capital city. States also have state symbols.

To the south is Oregon. Idaho lies to the east. The Pacific Ocean is to the west.

Washington is famous for its big evergreen forests. The state also has deserts and prairies.

The Cascade Range stretches more than 700 miles (1,100 km).

The mountains of the Cascade Range run down the middle of Washington, dividing the western and eastern parts of the state.

Washington's Animals

Washington is home to many animals. Salmon swim in Washington's many lakes and rivers. Bears and elk roam the forests and mountains. Near the coast, orcas and gray whales look for food.

The climates of western and eastern Washington are very different. In the eastern part of the state, winters are cold and snowy. Summers tend to be very hot. Western Washington has a milder climate. It does not get very hot or cold. But it does get a lot of rain. Winter tends to be the region's wettest season. In December and January, it can rain more than 20 days each month!

Explore Online

Visit the website below. Does it give any new information about Washington's wildlife that wasn't in Chapter One?

Washington's Wildlife

abdocorelibrary.com/discovering-washington

Today, there are more than 10,000 members of the Yakama Nation.

CHAPTER 2

The People of Washington

American Indians were the first people to live in Washington. Today, there are 29 federally recognized American Indian nations in the state. Eastern Washington has been home to the Colville and Spokane nations for thousands of years.

Sacagawea, *right*, helped William Clark, *left*, and Meriwether Lewis, *center*, journey more than 5,000 miles (8,000 km).

The Quinault nation lives on the coast. The Yakama are native to central Washington.

In 1805, Meriwether Lewis and William Clark arrived in Washington. They were sent by President Thomas Jefferson to explore the West.

What's in a Name?

The state of Washington was named after George Washington. Washington was the first president of the United States. The state's flag has an image of the president. So does the state seal.

Washington's state flag was adopted in 1923.

Sacagawea, a Shoshone woman, helped the explorers communicate with the native nations.

Lewis and Clark published the story of their journey in 1814. People were fascinated. Some decided to move west to Washington.

Many of the **settlers** stole land from American Indian nations. They also brought diseases that killed many American Indian people.

Today, only 2 percent of people in Washington are American Indian. About 65 percent are white, and 14 percent are Hispanic or Latino. Almost 11 percent are Asian. Nearly 5 percent are Black.

Culture

Music is an important part of Washington's culture. Many iconic musicians are from Washington. Jimi Hendrix was one of them. He was a guitarist in the 1960s. Kurt Cobain was also from Washington. His band Nirvana became famous during the 1990s.

The Seattle Seahawks won their first Super Bowl title in 2014.

Sports are also important in Washington. Many people cheer for the Seattle Seahawks football team. The Sounders soccer team, the Mariners baseball team, and the Kraken hockey team are popular too.

Boeing's airplane manufacturing plant in Everett, Washington, is the largest factory in the world.

Industries

Many businesses were founded in Washington. Boeing, a company that makes airplanes, was founded in 1916. During the 1970s, Bill Gates and

Microsoft's headquarters are in Redmond, Washington.

Steve Ballmer began a computer company called Microsoft. Today, it's the second-largest company in the world. In 1994, Jeff Bezos founded an online shopping company called Amazon. The headquarters for Microsoft and Amazon are still in the state.

Washington produces more blueberries than any other state in the country.

Farming is another important **industry** in Washington. The state has more than 35,000 farms. Many farmers grow fruits and vegetables. Some raise livestock. Altogether, the state's farms make more than $10 billion every year.

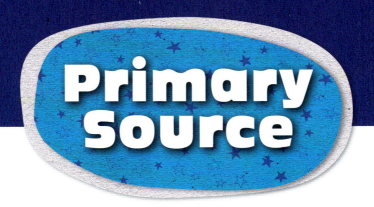

Primary Source

Daniel Stewart is a member of the Spokane nation. He explains what life was like for the Spokane people before Europeans arrived:

> The Spokanes were a **semi-nomadic** tribe who lived off the region's major rivers. . . . The river provided the main source of **sustenance**, primarily in the form of salmon. . . .

Source: "Renewing Indigenous Economies: An Interview with Daniel Stewart, Spokane Tribe." *YouTube*, uploaded by PolicyEd, 23 Apr. 2020, youtube.com. Accessed 8 Jan. 2024.

What's the Big Idea?

Read this quote. What's the main idea? Explain how the main idea is supported by details.

Olympia became the capital of Washington in 1853.

CHAPTER 3

Places in Washington

Olympia is the capital of Washington. The city has several protected natural areas. One of these areas is the Billy Frank Jr. Nisqually National Wildlife **Refuge**. The refuge is home to at least 250 types of birds. It also has several miles of hiking trails.

It takes 41 seconds for the Space Needle's elevator to bring people to the top of the tower.

Though Olympia has a lot to see, it is not one of Washington's most **populated** cities. It is not even in the top 20.

Seattle is Washington's most populated city. It is home to almost 750,000 people.

The Chihuly Garden and Glass museum displays the work of Dale Chihuly.

Many tourists come to Seattle to see the Space Needle. The Space Needle is a massive tower. It was built for the World's Fair in 1962. It is 605 feet (184 m) tall. Standing at the top, visitors get a 360-degree view of the city and the surrounding landscape. Seattle also has many museums. One popular museum is the Museum of Pop Culture. Chihuly Garden and Glass is another famous museum.

Mount Rainier is an active volcano, but it hasn't had a big eruption in 500 years.

Parks

Washington is home to three national parks. One of the most popular is Mount Rainier National Park. The park protects the land around Mount Rainier, the tallest mountain in Washington. People come to the park to hike the mountain and see the wildflowers growing on its slopes.

Olympic National Park is also popular. It is located in western Washington. The park

Olympic National Park is home to many tall rock formations called sea stacks.

covers nearly 1 million acres (405,000 ha) of the Olympic **Peninsula**. Visitors can fish and explore the park's beaches.

Landmarks

Mount Saint Helens is an active volcano in southern Washington. It is 40,000 years old.

Mount Saint Helens and the area surrounding it is a national volcanic monument. People can explore the site's visitor center to learn about the volcano.

In eastern Washington, the Grand Coulee **Dam** is a major source of power. The dam turns running water from the Columbia River into electricity. It is the largest power source in the United States.

The 1980 Eruption of Mount Saint Helens

In May 1980, Mount Saint Helens erupted. It was the biggest volcanic eruption in US history. Lava and ash shot out of the volcano. In minutes, 230 square miles (595 sq km) around the mountain was destroyed. The eruption killed 57 people.

Mount Saint Helens is the most active volcano in the 48 connected states.

Washington is a beautiful and exciting place to live and visit. It has mountains, forests, and museums. The state has plenty to explore!

Further Evidence

Look at the website below. Does it give any new evidence to support Chapter Three?

Mount Saint Helens

abdocorelibrary.com/discovering-washington

State Map

KEY

 Capital   Park

 City or town   Point of interest

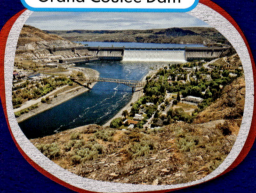
Grand Coulee Dam

Puget Sound

Washington: The Evergreen State

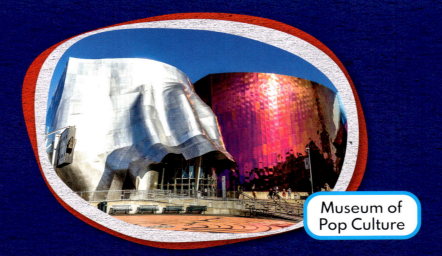

Museum of Pop Culture

Glossary

dam
a structure built across a body of water to hold water back

industry
a group of businesses that serve similar purposes

peninsula
an area of land surrounded by water on three sides

populated
settled or lived in

refuge
a sheltered or protected place

semi-nomadic
describing a group of people who live in temporary houses and move with the seasons, but who have a permanent place to which they return

settlers
people who moved to a new area

sustenance
things one needs to survive, such as food

Online Resources

To learn more about Washington, visit our free resource websites below.

Visit **abdocorelibrary.com** or scan this QR code for free Common Core resources for teachers and students, including vetted activities, multimedia, and booklinks, for deeper subject comprehension.

Visit **abdobooklinks.com** or scan this QR code for free additional online weblinks for further learning. These links are routinely monitored and updated to provide the most current information available.

Learn More

Abdo, Kenny. *Seattle Seahawks.* Abdo, 2022.

Payne, Stefanie. *The National Parks.* DK, 2020.

Tieck, Sarah. *Washington.* Abdo, 2020.

Index

Billy Frank Jr. Nisqually National Wildlife Refuge, 21

Cascade Range, 8
Chihuly Garden and Glass, 23
Columbia River, 26
Colville nation, 11

Grand Coulee Dam, 26

Mount Rainier National Park, 24
Mount Saint Helens, 25–26
Museum of Pop Culture, 23

Olympia, 7, 21–22
Olympic National Park, 24–25

Quinault nation, 12

Sacagawea, 13
Seattle, 5–6, 22–23
Space Needle, 23
Spokane nation, 11, 19

Washington, George, 12

Yakama Nation, 12

About the Author

Blythe Lawrence is a journalist from Seattle. She writes about sports and history.